# HEBREW GOLD

## Steven D. Nielsen

**HEBREW GOLD**
Copyright © 2025 by Steven D. Nielsen.

ISBN 979-8-89672-222-9 (paperback)
ISBN 979-8-89672-224-3 (hardback)
ISBN 979-8-89672-223-6 (ebook)

Because of the dynamic nature of the Internet, any web addresses or links contained in this book may have changed since publication and may no longer be valid. The views expressed in the work are solely those of the author and do not necessarily reflect the views of the publisher, and the publisher hereby disclaims any responsibility for them.

Printed in the United States of America.

PROMINENT
BOOKS

5830 E 2nd St, Ste 7000 #9983
Casper, Wyoming, 82609
USA

Special thanks to:
Richard G. Freeman
Carlos Jessurun, M.D.
Earl Silverstein

Dedicated to my wife Susan Y. Nielsen
And our children:
Patrick D. Nielsen
Michael D. Nielsen
Joelle Y. Greenhalgh
Joshua M. Nielsen
Jacob T. Nielsen

# INTRODUCTION

Forty-two years ago, a young Obstetrics and Gynecology Resident and friend of mine was the instructor of a men's group who met in an old Presbyterian church on 43rd street in Houston, Texas every Sabbath morning. Luckily, I was present on the day he presented the fascinating information you are about to enjoy.

This future physician had not only gathered a great deal of captivating data, but he presented it so well that morning that he left his listeners spellbound. Time passed and I came to know him well. He was unpretentious, strikingly handsome, tall, and with a full head of dark-brown hair. His hands and fingers were strong and graceful and could not only set a piano keyboard aflame with the music of Frederic Chopin and Ludwig Von Beethoven, but deliver tiny babies into this harsh world safely. Plus, in a touch- football game at a father's and Son's Campout one weekend he threw the football like Joe Montana!

Jonathan Hulme is the name of this humble and talented individual. He is the father of eight children and twenty-four grandchildren but tragically at this time in his life he is battling Lymphoma. Back when I first met Jonathan, he was full of health and vitality and extremely busy with studies and a budding family. Back then he usually made hospital rounds on less than four hours of sleep per night, but excelled in his specialty, passing his boards with high marks. Yet during this hectic time he always presented well-prepared and detailed lessons in our weekly men's meetings and especially so with the subject of this book.

What you are about to read was so intriguing that on the day Jonathan introduced the subject he had our men's class sitting on the edge of our chairs with our eyes and ears wide open! My modest friend's presentation included overhead slides and reprints from experts on Hebrew text and in the many years since, I have also gathered additional supporting data from a host of reliable sources. These include the writings of Hebrew scholars, public records, the internet and of course, the scriptures themselves - the meat of which comprise this book. I have also given four public presentations on the material in the past but other projects including a five novel Historical Fiction series and two other works of fiction took my attention away for a time.

One year has passed since my last presentation but not long ago the curiosity of another close Christian friend, - also a quasi-Hebrew scholar, caused me to blow the dust from my old overhead slides and reprints on Hebrew writing styles. I also did additional research and then recorded much of the information on Power Point for sharing in seminars. Now in book form this compelling information is professionally researched, highly enlightening and vital to opening the understandings of a most important prophesy found in Ezekiel regarding the uniting of sacred volumes of Holy writ.

## Ezekiel 37: 16 & 17

"Moreover, thou son of man, take thee one stick, and write upon it, For Judah, and for the children of Israel his companions:

then take another stick, and write upon it, For Joseph, the stick of Ephraim and for all the house of Israel his companions:

and join them one to another into one stick; and they shall become one in thine hand."

## And then... Ezekiel 37:18, 19 & 20

"And when the children of thy people shall speak unto thee, saying, Wilt thou not shew us what thou *meanest* by these?

Say unto them, Thus saith the Lord God; Behold, I will take the stick of Joseph, which *is* in the hand of Ephraim, and the tribes of Israel his fellows, and will put them with him, even with the stick of Judah,

and make them one stick, and they shall be one in mine hand.

And the sticks whereon thou writest shall be in thine hand before their eyes."

The scriptural inference here is clear that God commanded the prophets to compile sacred records for the blessings of two separate groups of people by using the medium common in those ancient times, - papyrus and the <u>sticks</u> whereon the papyrus was rolled - to record and to teach His commandments to these two separate peoples. - So, who are these two groups of people<u>? Judah, the children of Israel his companions *and* Joseph, the House of Israel his companions.</u>

Furthermore, it is also abundantly clear that these two peoples both sprang from the House of Israel. **But exactly who were they and where did they live?**

# JESUS THE CHRIST

What you are about to read while not directly about the Lord Jesus Christ or His life, gives constant reference to Him throughout. He it was who atoned for the sins of **all** the peoples of the world and not just those who were living relatively close to the place of His birth or vast parts of the Eastern Hemisphere where He and His followers first proclaimed the gospel.

Christ was and is the God of the *entire Earth* and every man, woman and child who ever lived upon it or who yet will, will even-

1

tually come to understand that His undying love and unbelievable sacrifice was and is for them. This book then is about all the peoples of the earth, those of the Eastern and likewise those of the Western Hemisphere and the Word of the Lord to them all.

**John 3:16 & 17 - "For God so loved the world, that he gave his only begotten Son, that whosoever believeth in him should not perish, but have everlasting life.**

**For God sent not his Son into the world to condemn the world; but that the world through him might be saved."**

## The Stick of Judah

What is the Stick of Judah? And what exactly is this Hebrew Gold and where can we find it? - Answers to these questions are to be found in this book, in the writings to be shown clearly revealed in their original configuration.

## To begin with, the Holy Bible is the Stick of Judah

God's revelations were recorded by Hebrew prophets on papyrus scrolls yet today many people do not know from whence the Bible comes, or even who wrote it.

*"...they shall have a Bible; and it shall proceed forth from the Jews, mine ancient covenant people. And what thank they the Jews for the Bible which they receive from them? Yea, what do the Gentiles mean? Do they remember the travails, and the labors, and the pains of the Jews, and their diligence unto me, in bringing forth salvation unto the Gentiles?"* - 2 Nephi 29:4

# The Holy Bible is a Gift from the Jews

Hebrew prophets who recorded revelations from God within the pages of the Holy Bible were more than likely trained in an exclusive writing style. Today in modern times that ancient and unique writing style is called…

## CHIASMUS
(kī'azməs)

## What is a Chiasmus?

Well-planned word patterns and diagrams within verses, paragraphs, chapters, even entire books; Chiasmus' are structured phrases that took deep thought and planning in their development. In addition, Chiasmus' are teachings strengthened by repetition of ideas and contrasts of concepts, the result of which can be pleasing, even poetic, a song to the ear and amazingly effective in the teaching and learning and recalling process. The following are a few basic beginning examples:

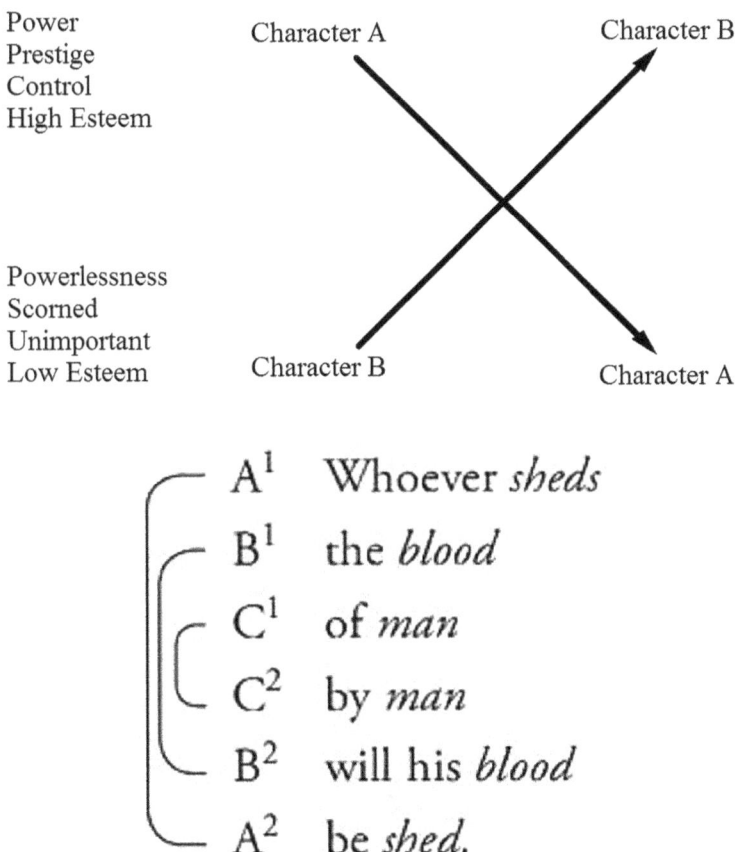

**Alternate and related Terms:**
Chiasm
Chiastic Structure
Concentric Symmetry
Chiastically
Inverted Parallelism
Reverse Symmetry

Below is a pictorial of a chiasmus laid out in a parallel diagram.

(A) My son, give ear to my WORDS (1)
  (B) KEEP THE COMMANDMENTS of God and ye shall PROSPER IN THE LAND (1)
    (C) DO AS I HAVE DONE (2)
      (D) in REMEMBERING THE CAPTIVITY of our fathers (2);
        (E) for they were in BONDAGE (2)
          (F) he surely did DELIVER them (2)
            (G) TRUST in God (3)
              (H) supported in their TRIALS, and TROUBLES, and AFFLICTIONS (3)
                (I) shall be lifted up at the LAST DAY (3)
                  (J) I KNOW this not of myself but of GOD (4)
                    (K) BORN OF GOD (5)
                      (L) I sought to destroy the church of God (6-9)
                        (M) MY LIMBS were paralyzed (10)
                          (N) Fear of being in the PRESENCE OF GOD (14-15)
                            (O) PAINS of a damned soul (16)
                              (P) HARROWED UP BY THE MEMORY OF SINS (17)
                                (Q) I remembered JESUS CHRIST, SON OF GOD (17)
                                (Q') I cried, JESUS, SON OF GOD (18)
                              (P') HARROWED UP BY THE MEMORY OF SINS no more
                            (O') Joy as exceeding as was the PAIN (18)
                          (N') Long to be in the PRESENCE OF GOD (22)
                        (M') My LIMBS received their strength again (23)
                      (L') I labored to bring souls to repentance (24)
                    (K') BORN OF GOD (26)
                  (J') Therefore MY KNOWLEDGE IS OF GOD (26)
                (I') and RAISE ME UP AT THE LAST DAY (28)
              (H') supported under TRIALS, TROUBLES, and AFFLICTIONS (27)
            (G') TRUST in him (27)
          (F') He will deliver me (27)
        (E') As God brought our fathers out of BONDAGE and captivity (28-29)
      (D') Retain in REMEMBRANCE THEIR CAPTIVITY (28-29)
    (C') I KNOW AS I DO KNOW (30)
  (B') KEEP THE COMMANDMENTS and ye shall PROSPER IN THE LAND (30)
(A') This is according to his WORD (30).

## Chiasmus – origins

The term is derived from the Greek, "crossing," or "X" and its root comes from the letter "chi," the 22nd letter of the Greek alphabet. Symbolic of a rhetorical literary feature in grammatical constructions, the letter X helps readers to imagine repetition of concepts in reverse order, or with reverse meaning:

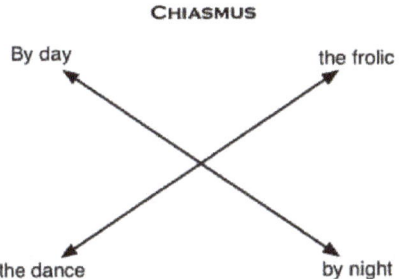

*Thou has made the earth to tremble; thou hast broken it: heal the breaches thereof; for it shaketh." - Psalms 60:2 (KJV)*

Key phrases form a mental "X" Chiasticly.

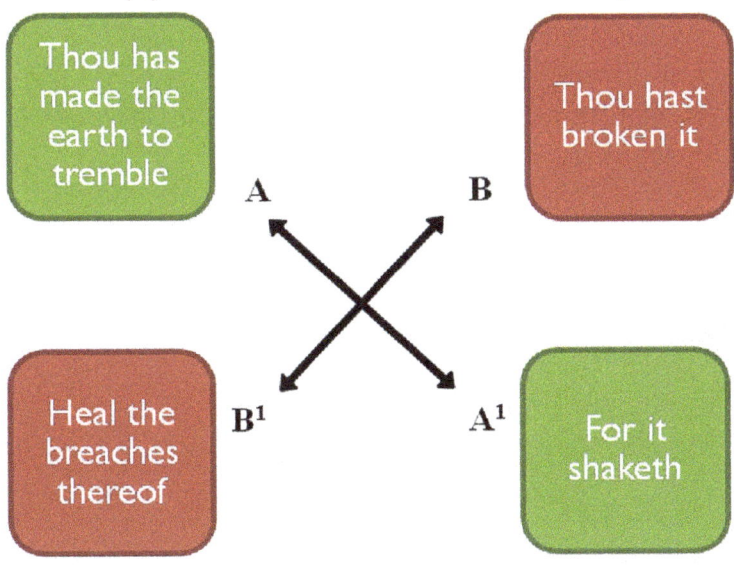

*Mark 2 vs. 27*

| | |
|---|---|
| A | The Sabbath |
| B | was made for man |
| B' | and not man |
| A' | for the sabbath |

A        B

B'      A'

With the two preceding simple examples - with more complex Chiasmus' to follow - enter…

## Professor Nils Wilhelm Lund

Dr. Lund was born in Gavle, Sweden in 1885 and died in 1954. As a child, his family immigrated to Argentina where he grew to maturity and eventually became renowned for twenty-two literary works and forty-six publications all available in three languages. Lund's works are still referenced throughout the world.

Extraordinarily little, if anything, was known about the presence of Chiasmus in the Holy Bible until Nils Lund's extensive research of the Greek and King James versions revealed them. Laboring from 1931 on through 1941 he carefully searched for and unfolded scores of scriptures replete with Chiastic style.

A dedicated biblical scholar, after meticulously diagramming many key bible passages from both Old and New Testaments of the Greek and King James Bibles, his book - "Chiasmus in the New Testament" - was finally published in 1942.

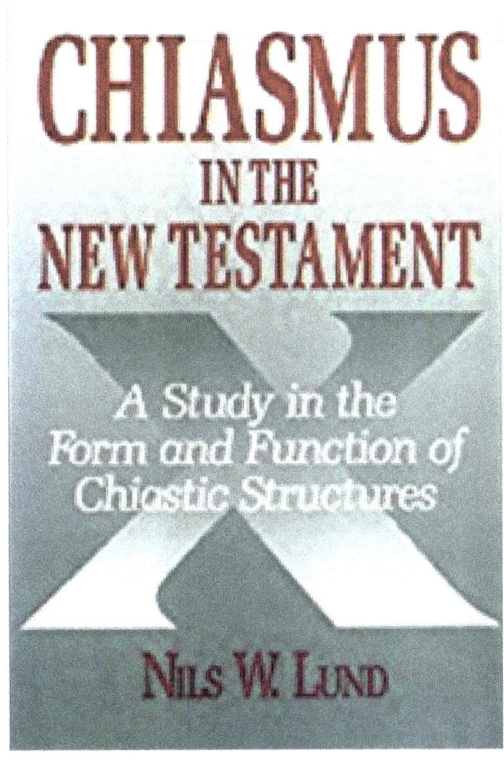

# Parallelism

## Complex Chiasmus are best revealed diagramed in a parallel presentation

### Five basic goals:

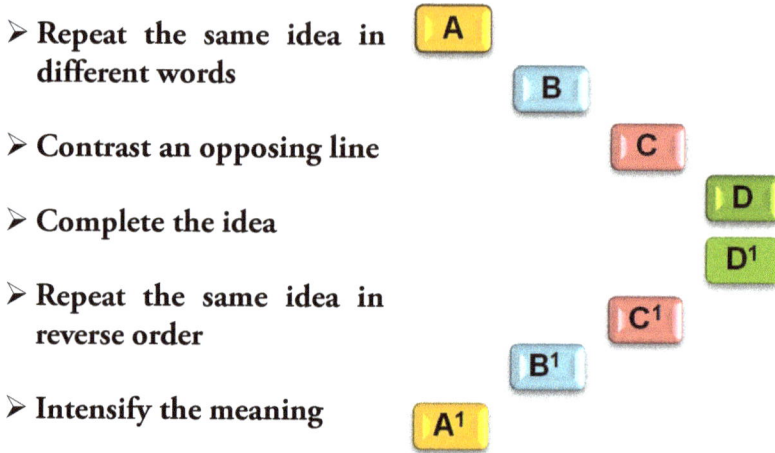

- ➤ Repeat the same idea in different words

- ➤ Contrast an opposing line

- ➤ Complete the idea

- ➤ Repeat the same idea in reverse order

- ➤ Intensify the meaning

**For example: Psalms 3: vs 7- 8 (from the Greek Bible)**

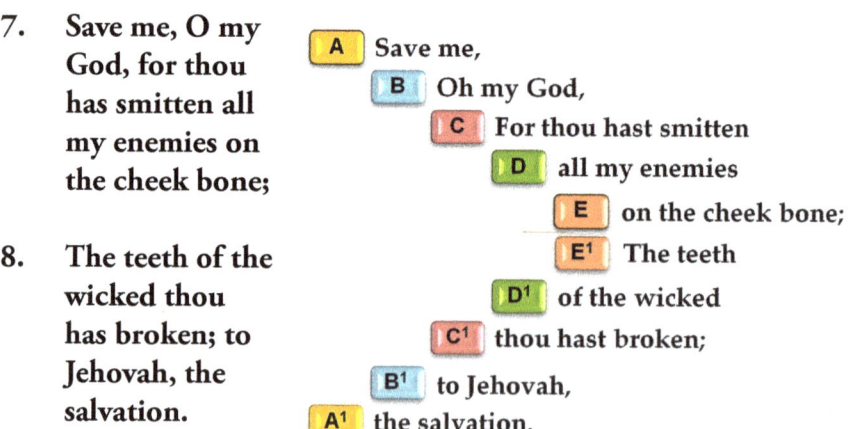

7.   Save me, O my God, for thou has smitten all my enemies on the cheek bone;

8.   The teeth of the wicked thou has broken; to Jehovah, the salvation.

Note how: A, A' - B, B' - C, C' etc. intensify the message of the scripture bringing it to sharp focus in the center, E, E.'

10

**Genesis 7:21-23 (Greek Bible)**

21. And all flesh died that moved upon the earth, both of fowl, and of cattle, and of beast, and of every creeping thing that creepeth upon the earth, and every man:
22. All in whose nostrils was the breath of life, of all that was in the dry land, died.
23. And every living substance was destroyed which was upon the face of the ground, both man, and cattle, and the creeping things, and the fowl of the heaven; and they were destroyed from the earth: and Noah only remained alive, and they that were with him in the ark.

Try to identify the parallel pattern of the above scripture's verses before viewing the diagram below. Fairly difficult is it not? Most definitely therefore it is somewhat of a miracle that Bible scholars like Dr. Lund discovered Chiasmus in the first place. Again, contrast A, A' - B, B' - C, C' all the way to G, G.'

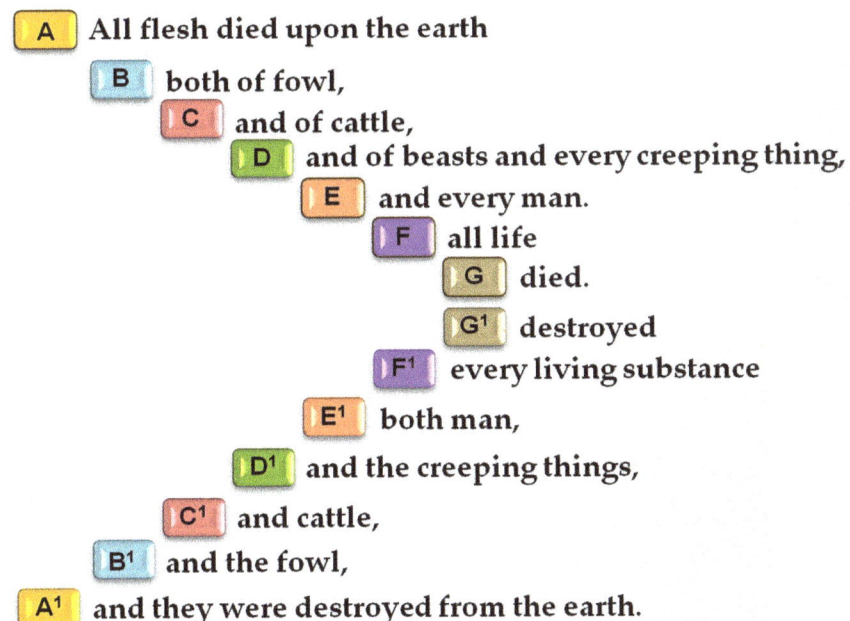

   **A**   **All flesh died upon the earth**
      **B**   **both of fowl,**
        **C**   **and of cattle,**
          **D**   **and of beasts and every creeping thing,**
            **E**   **and every man.**
              **F**   **all life**
                **G**   **died.**
                **G¹**   **destroyed**
              **F¹**   **every living substance**
            **E¹**   **both man,**
          **D¹**   **and the creeping things,**
        **C¹**   **and cattle,**
      **B¹**   **and the fowl,**
   **A¹**   **and they were destroyed from the earth.**

In today's complex societies, the more a message, theme, idea, or teaching is presented in media or print, the more likely it is to be remembered. Just as in olden times, repetition is essential in the learning and remembering process. Facts are that consumers must hear or see an advertiser's message a minimum of seven times before they will even try the product or service in question.

It was no different in ancient times. Therefore, wise teachers, scholars and especially prophets from Hebrew backgrounds learned to repeat and to emphasize key segments of their messages within sentences, paragraphs, chapters, and even entire books! They knew that <u>recall follows repetition.</u> Thus, the advent of the rhythmic, poetic, repetitious, chiastic style.

## Psalms 124:7 (King James Version)

7.   **Our soul is escaped as a bird out of the snare of the fowlers: the snare is broken, and we are escaped.**

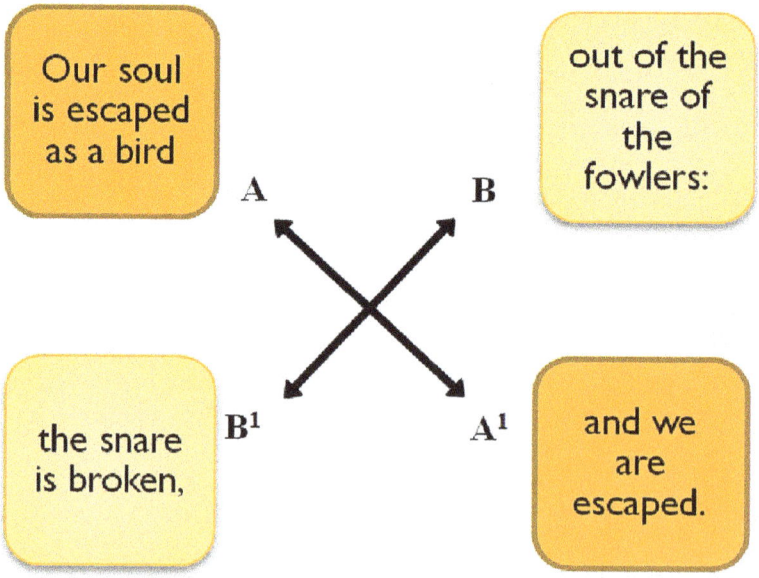

# Psalms 58:1-11 (KJV)

1. Do ye indeed speak righteousness, O congregation? do ye judge uprightly, O ye sons of men?
2. Yea, in heart ye work wickedness; ye weigh the violence of your hands in the earth.
3. The wicked are estranged from the womb: they go astray as soon as they be born, speaking lies.
4. Their poison *is* like the poison of a serpent: *they are* like the deaf adder *that* stoppeth her ear;
5. Which will not hearken to the voice of charmers, charming never so wisely.
6. Break their teeth, O God, in their mouth: break out the great teeth of the young lions, O Lord.
7. Let them melt away as waters *which* run continually: *when* he bendeth *his bow to shoot* his arrows, let them be as cut in pieces.
8. As a snail *which* melteth, let *every one of them* pass away: *like* the *untimely birth of a woman, *that* they may not see the sun.
9. Before your pots can feel the thorns, he shall take them away as with a whirlwind, both living, and in *his* wrath.
10. The righteous shall rejoice when he seeth the vengeance: he shall wash his feet in the blood of the wicked.
11. So that a man shall say, Verily *there is* a reward for the righteous: verily he is a God that judgeth in the earth.

* The Greek Bible uses the word <u>abortions</u> instead of the gentler words; <u>untimely birth</u>, and thus we begin to see that even King James scholars changed some key words and even whole meanings in their translations; regardless and fortunately, however, many Chiasmus' survived their work. - The King James Version being closest to the original Hebrew and Greek is the bible most commonly used by people today; this author references it often.

# Psalms 58:1-11 (Diagrammed)

**A** Do ye indeed speak righteousness, O congregation? Do ye judge uprightly, O ye sons of men?

**B** Yea, in heart ye work wickedness, ye weigh out the violence of your hands in the earth.

**C** The wicked are estranged from the womb:

**D** Their poison is like the poison of a serpent:

**E** Break their teeth, O God, in their mouth:

**E¹** break out the great teeth of the young lions, O Lord.

**D¹** Let them melt away as waters, as a snail which melteth,

**C¹** like the untimely birth of a woman, that they may not see the sun.

**B¹** The righteous shall rejoice when he seeth vengeance: he shall wash his feet in the blood of the wicked.

**A¹** So that a man shall say, there is a reward for the righteous: Verily he is a God that judgeth in the earth.

Source: John W. Welch, BYU Studies Autumn 1969

The scripture is obviously well thought out, well balanced and repetitious with the crucial point – E and E' making it clear that the author, in this case David, strongly desires God to punish the wicked.

Using the writing style, he had been trained to use throughout his life, the young king makes his point and thoroughly informs the reader.

# Psalms 59:1-17 (KJV Bible)

1. Deliver me from mine enemies, O my God: defend me from them that rise up against me.

2. Deliver me from the workers of iniquity, and save me from bloody men.

3. For, lo, they lie in wait for my soul: the mighty are gathered against me; not for my transgression, nor for my sin, O Lord.

4. They run and prepare themselves without my fault: awake to help me, and behold.

5. Thou therefore, O Lord God of hosts, the God of Israel, awake to visit all the heathen: be not merciful to any wicked transgressors. Selah.

6. They return at evening: they make a noise like a dog, and go round about the city.

7. Behold, they belch out with their mouth: swords are in their lips: for who, say they, doth hear?

8. But thou, O Lord, shalt laugh at them; thou shalt have all the heathen in derision.

9. Because of his strength will I wait upon thee: for God is my defense.

10. The God of my mercy shall prevent me: God shall let me see my desire upon mine enemies.

11. Slay them not, lest my people forget: scatter them by thy power and bring them down, O Lord our shield.

12. For the sin of their mouth and the words of their lips let them even be taken in their pride: and for cursing and lying which they speak.

13. Consume them in wrath, consume them, that they may not be: and let them know that God ruleth in Jacob unto the ends of the earth. Selah.

14. And at evening let them return; and let them make a noise like a dog, and go round about the city.

15. Let them wander up and down for meat, and grudge if they be not satisfied.

16. But I will sing of thy power; yea, I will sing aloud of thy mercy in the morning: for thou hast been my defense and refuge in the day of my Trouble.

17. Unto thee, O my strength, will I sing: for God is my defense, and the God of my mercy."

# Psalms 59:1-17 (Diagrammed)

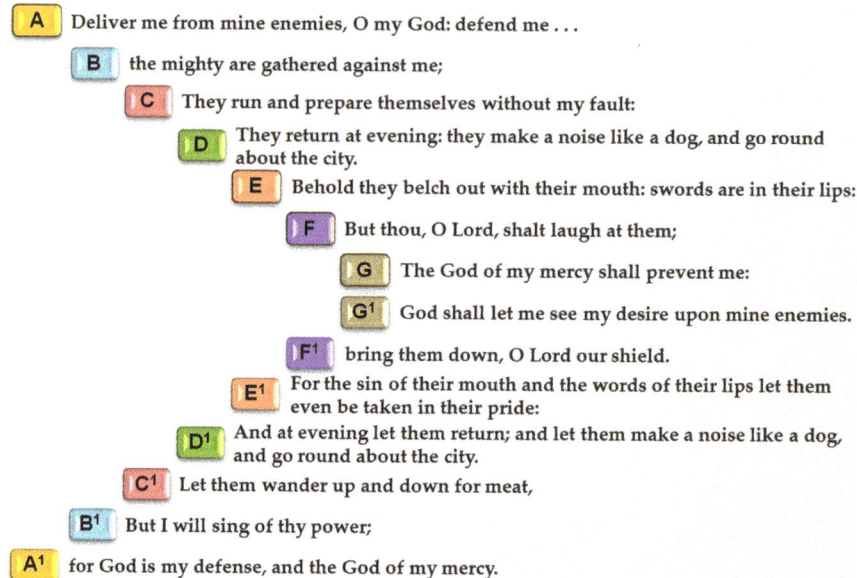

A — Deliver me from mine enemies, O my God: defend me . . .

B — the mighty are gathered against me;

C — They run and prepare themselves without my fault:

D — They return at evening: they make a noise like a dog, and go round about the city.

E — Behold they belch out with their mouth: swords are in their lips:

F — But thou, O Lord, shalt laugh at them;

G — The God of my mercy shall prevent me:

G¹ — God shall let me see my desire upon mine enemies.

F¹ — bring them down, O Lord our shield.

E¹ — For the sin of their mouth and the words of their lips let them even be taken in their pride:

D¹ — And at evening let them return; and let them make a noise like a dog, and go round about the city.

C¹ — Let them wander up and down for meat,

B¹ — But I will sing of thy power;

A¹ — for God is my defense, and the God of my mercy.

(Source: John W. Welch, BYU Studies Autumn 1969)

Only 16 Bible Chiasmus' are shown and explained in this work, but the Holy Bible contains hundreds of examples within its pages. The Book of Isaiah alone has over 1,000 poetic examples! – And since Dr. Nils W. Lund's exhaustive work in the 1930's and 1940's dozens of Bible scholars have added technical insight.

## Stop and Consider . . .

➤ Obviously, such carefully composed composition, sentence, and paragraph structures were no accident.

➤ An elevated level of planning and preparation must have been required before prophets applied ink to papyrus.

➤ Did they begin in the center and work backwards?

➤ Did they begin with the top and bottom sentences and work toward the middle?

➤ Moses and David were more than likely trained in the Hebrew chiastic writing technique as well as all Hebrew prophets.

➤ Regardless of how they occurred, it took great wisdom, skill, and time to write and construct sentences, paragraphs, chapters, and especially entire books of scripture written in Chiastic patterns.

Certainly, Hebrew scholars and teachers of the day were well aware of the poetic flavor, subtle beauty, emphasis, reverse order, and repetition within certain scriptures, but did they purposely structure and create them? In my opinion some Chiasmus' are so vast, so complex and deeply profound that they would have taken mortal man, weeks, months or even years to construct.

The mind and the education of man certainly played a roll, but I know that the revelations recorded by God's holy prophets are true, authoritative instructions, insights, blessings, and needed direction carefully recorded exactly as received. The prophets then passed them on to us in holy writ, or scripture!

Continuing on, please consider the following scripture presented in a compound Chiasmus…

## Ezekiel 34:5-6 (from the Greek Bible)

**"And they were scattered, because there is no shepherd: and they became meat to all the beasts of the field, when they were scattered.**

My sheep wandered through all the mountains, and upon every high hill: yea, my flock was scattered upon all the face of the earth and none did search or seek after them."

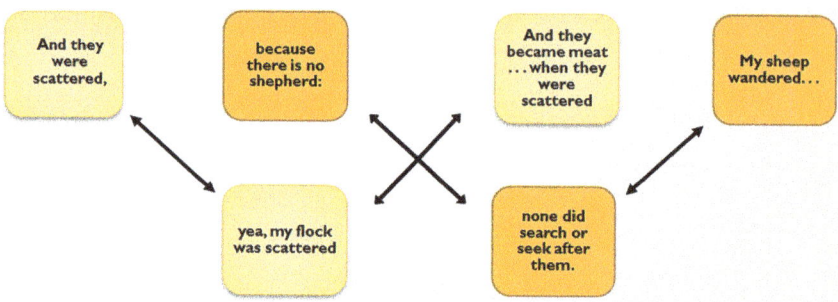

## Are Chiasmus' only found in the Old Testament?

➢ Also prevalent throughout the New Testament.

➢ More easily recognized in original Hebrew.

➢ Subsequent translations and revisions of the Holy Bible have proven unfriendly to basic chiastic structures.

➢ Subsequent translations and revisions of the scriptures have muted or even destroyed their original meaning and also the poetic/rhythmic, and chiastic flavor.

➢ Furthermore, modern translations and revisions often further weaken the original message and prophetic intent.

➢ Pure Chiasmus' seem to be limited exclusively to Hebrew writ, especially within Holy Scripture.

# Hebrew Influence on the Lord Jesus Christ...

**Christ was raised in a Hebrew home**

**As a youth Christ taught Jewish Elders in the Temple**

Paintings beautifully portray scenes from the Holy Bible, but sadly precious little is known about the youth, adolescence, and young adult life of our Savior Jesus Christ. Unfortunately, the scriptures themselves are virtually silent regarding his formative years but we can rest assured that an old Hebrew saying: "In every home a Jewish mother," described Mary, his youthful mother, perfectly.

As we know, Mary was a chosen vessel. Reared under a strict Hebrew upbringing herself, she was most likely intelligent, chaste, honest, thrifty and an industrious woman. Chosen by God our Heavenly Father to be the earthly mother of Christ, she knew the weight of her responsibility well and it simply goes without saying that Mary provided diligent nurturing, true love, pure example, and careful instruction to her precious son.

And the same must be said of Joseph, Christ's earthly father and guide. In addition to the Son of God, Joseph and Mary became the parents of several additional children and we can only believe that due to necessity, there were household chores, rules, structure, and discipline for all their children, including young Jesus. Mary and Joseph's teachings, coupled with Hebrew schooling in classrooms and synagogues plus being taught the difficult trade of carpentering by his humble earthly father gives no doubt that our Lord received a spiritual, physical, practical, and thoroughly well-rounded education.

The young Lord of all probably even learned the poetic, rhythmic, and complex writing style of the Hebrew (Chiasmus) but no actual document written by His hand survives. Fortunately, His compassionate and powerful all-encompassing teachings were recorded by holy apostles and prophets of God, then printed out and finally made available to humanity.

Continuing through the New Testament then, the following are a few teachings of Christ; scripture, richly flavored with the Hebrew poetic writing technique of repetition and intensification found throughout:

# Luke 16:13 (KJV)

13. No servant can serve two masters: for either he will hate the one, and love the other; or else he will hold to the one, and despise the other. Ye cannot serve God and mammon.

> **A** No servant can serve two masters:
>> **B** for either he will hate the one,
>>> **C** and love the other;
>>> **C¹** or else he will hold to the one,
>> **B¹** and despise the other.
> **A¹** Ye cannot serve God and mammon.

# Matthew 5:23-24 (KJV)

23. Therefore if thou bring thy gift to the altar, and there rememberest that thy brother hath ought against thee;
24. Leave there thy gift before the altar, and go thy way; first be reconciled to thy brother, and then come and offer thy gift.

> **A** Therefore if thou bring thy gift to the altar,
>> **B** and there rememberest that thy brother hath ought against thee;
>>> **C** Leave there thy gift before the altar,
>>> **C¹** and go thy way;
>> **B¹** first be reconciled to thy brother,
> **A¹** and then come and offer thy gift.

# Matthew 7:6 (KJV)

6. Give not that which is holy unto the dogs, neither cast ye your pearls before swine, lest they trample them under their feet, and turn again and rend you

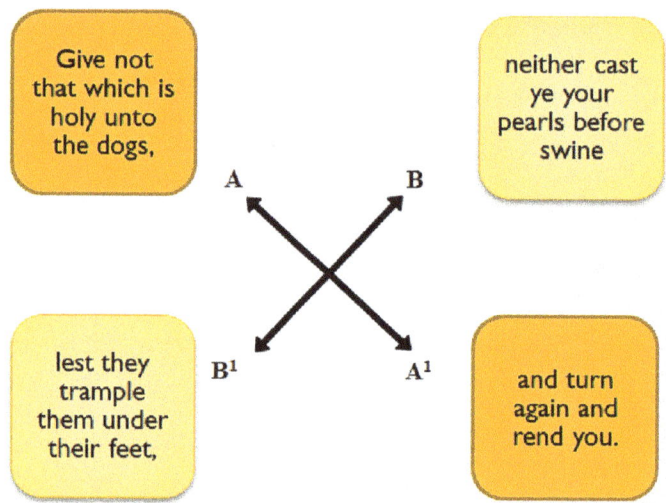

# Matthew 13:15 (KJV)

15. For this people's heart is waxed gross, and *their* ears are dull of hearing, and their eyes have closed; lest at any time they should see with *their* eyes, and hear with *their* ears, and should understand with *their* heart, and should be converted, and I should heal them.

**A** For this people's <u>heart</u> is waxed gross,

    **B** and *their* <u>ears</u> are dull of hearing,

        **C** and their <u>eyes</u> they have closed;

        **C¹** lest at any time they should see with *their* <u>eyes</u>,

    **B¹** and hear with *their* <u>ears</u>,

**A¹** and should understand with *their* <u>heart</u>,

# John 1:1-2 (KJV)

1. In the beginning was the Word, and the Word was with God, and the Word was God.
2. The same was in the beginning with God.

> **A** In the beginning
>> **B** was
>>> **C** the Word, and the Word
>>>> **D** was with God,
>>>> **D¹** and the Word was God.
>>> **C¹** The same (referring to the Word)
>> **B¹** was
> **A¹** in the beginning with God.

# 1 John 3:9 (KJV)

9. Whosoever is born of God doth not commit sin; for his seed remaineth in him: and he cannot sin, because he is born of God.

> **A** Whosoever is born of God
>> **B** doth not commit sin;
>>> **C** for his seed remaineth in him:
>> **B¹** and he cannot sin,
> **A¹** because he is born of God.

## *Part of an Epistle of Paul the Apostle to the Hebrews:*

## *Chapter 12: Vs. 1-2 (KJV)*

1. Wherefore seeing we also are compassed about with so great a cloud of witnesses, let us lay aside every weight, and the sin which doth so easily beset us, and let us run with patience the race that is set before us,

2. Looking unto Jesus the author and finisher of our faith; who for the joy that was set before him endured the cross, despising the shame, and is set down at the right hand of the throne of God

### Hebrews 12:1-2 (Diagrammed)

**A** we are <u>compassed about</u> with so great a cloud of witnesses,

  **B** let us lay aside every weight, and the <u>sin</u> which doth so easily beset us.

    **C** and let us run with <u>patience</u>

      **D** the race that is <u>set before us</u>.

        **E** Looking unto <u>Jesus the author</u>

        **E¹** and <u>finisher</u> of our faith;

      **D¹** who for the joy that was <u>set before him</u>

    **C¹** <u>endured</u> the cross,

  **B¹** despising the <u>shame</u>.

**A¹** and is <u>set down</u> at the right hand of the throne of God.

Note: Until the Lord Jesus Christ called Paul into the ministry on the road to Damascus he was known as Saul of Tarsus, a Jewish Pharisee, who zealously persecuted Christians. Saul (Paul) was also raised a Hebrew.

A prolific writer, Paul became a dynamic apostle and prophet of God and his letters to the various churches throughout the middle east clearly reveal his Hebrew background, education and writing style (Chiasmus).

Paul's Hebrew (Jewish or Judaic) background and writing styles throughout the Holy Bible provide powerful evidence that the Bible is the very _Stick of Judah_. The question now becomes which English version of the Holy Bible is the most accurate, the closest to the original Hebrew text?

## James VI King of Scotland who became
## James I King of England & Ireland

King James was born June 19, 1566 (Died March 27, 1625) and his gift to the world - The King James Version of the Holy Bible is a miracle in and of itself. With strict ground rules limiting translation to the original Hebrew, and Greek Bibles, plus slight influence from the Geneva and other English Bibles, and for his own aggrandizement, James authorized the version in a.d.1604. Costly even by today's standards, the King had fifty-four (54) brilliant bible scholars hired including Puritan clergy and other high-ranking Churchmen, and the work began.

Among these notables were Lancelot Andrews, Dean of Westminster, George Abbot, a brilliant author, along with some seasoned Arabic scholars and two expert mathematicians. Divided into six carefully balanced committees, they labored for seven years eventually approving and printing the final copies of the King James version for public use in the year 1611.

Minor grammatical errors were corrected as years went by but regardless, by 1650 the King James Bible became the scriptural standard of excellence and was widely read throughout Great Britain and her vast provinces.

Because of its foundation being true to the original Hebrew and Greek Bibles, hundreds of the passages are rich in Chiastic structure and flavor and providentially preserved within the pages of the King James Version.

Tragically, modern day revisions to the four hundred- and seven-year-old King James Bible have damaged and even destroyed the meaning and beauty of certain passages that trained scholars had so painstakingly translated from the original Hebrew and Greek languages.

For example, and as shown on the next two pages, carefully compare the following familiar scripture; 1 Corinthians 13: 8-13 when diagrammed Chiasticly.

The first example is text from the New International Version of the Bible and on the opposite page the original King James Version. Note clear examples of damage and weakened meaning in the NIV compared to the King James Version:

# 1 Corinthians 13:8-13
## - a chiastic comparison -
# (New International Version)

**A** Love never ends

**B** But as for prophecies, they will come to an end; as for tongues, they will cease; as for knowledge, it will come to an end.

**C** For we know only in part, and we prophesy only in part, but when the complete comes, the partial will come to an end.

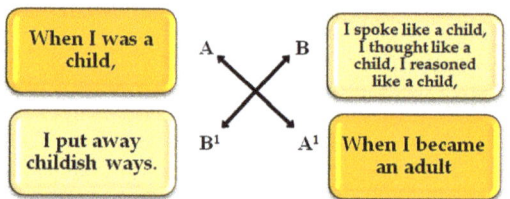

**C¹** For now we see in a mirror, dimly, but then we will see face to face. Now I know in part; then I will know fully, even as I have been fully known.

**B¹** And now faith, hope and love abide, these three

**A¹** And the greatest of these is love.

# 1 Corinthians 13:8-13
## - a chiastic comparison -
# (The King James Version)

**A** Charity <u>never faileth</u>:

    **B** but whether there be <u>prophecies</u>, they shall fail;

        **C** whether there be tongues, they shall cease;

        **C¹** Whether there be knowledge, it shall <u>vanish</u> away.

    **B¹** For we know in part, and we <u>prophesy</u> in part.

**A¹** But when that which is <u>perfect</u> is come, then that which is in part shall be done away.

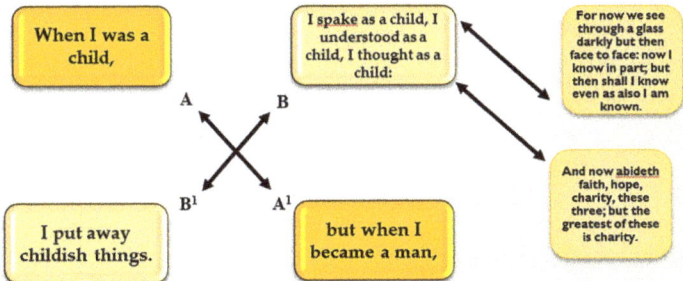

This careful comparison between the King James Version and the New International Version provides unmistakable evidence of how revisions to Holy Scripture not only damage chiastic structure but also mute or completely change the prophet/author's original intent and meaning.

For example, take the word charity. Charity is the pure love of Christ, powerful, all encompassing, without guile. Charity is God-like compassion for all humanity, etc. whereas the word love might describe one's feelings for pizza, or steak, a fine car and yes more poignantly the love of one's spouse or children. But charity on the other hand is love to the 10th power. It is forgiveness, humility, turning the other cheek, a deep desire to heal the sick, or giving one's own coat to a freezing stranger. The Lord Jesus Christ is charity personified.

Second examples: seeing through a glass darkly (KJV) versus looking into a mirror dimly (NIV), Paul was obviously referring to a person's own reflection being dark when compared with seeing another person such as himself face to face. Also, B and B' have little in common.

Another example: the author of 1 Corinthians was Paul the Apostle, a man. Yes, he became an adult, but not a woman adult. The above examples are minor you might say, and revisionists of the Holy Bible have probably meant well, but they were not prophets of God, nor did they (the revisionists) live during Old or New Testament times as did the original prophet/authors of the Hebrew and Greek bibles.

The original prophets lived and studied closely before and after the time of Christ and in fact wrote the word of God as they received it, through direct revelation from God! Words to teach humanity the ways of salvation; not wilted words from authors selling their wares at *worst* by trying not to offend or at *best* by using words to pacify and placate the reader.

And finally, as if the prophet authors of the Holy Bible wanted to leave us with an impressive (but challenging to read and understand) climax to their gift to humanity...

# The entire Book of Revelation is a Chiasmus!

(A) Prologue (1:1-20)
  (B) Seven Epistles (2:1-3:22)
    (C) Seven Seals (4:1-8:1)
      (D) 144,000 saints & Seven Trumpets (7:1-11:19)
        (E) The Two Witnesses (11:1-13)
          (F) Woman clothed with the sun (12:1)
            (G) Dragon in heaven (12:4)
              (H) Woman flees to wilderness (12:6)
                (I)  Satan cast out (12:12)
              (H$^1$) Woman flees to wilderness (12:14)
            (G$^1$) Dragon persecutes woman (12:15)
          (F$^1$) Woman's seed keeps the commandments of God (12:17)
        (E$^1$) The Two Beasts (13:1-18)
      (D$^1$) 144,000 saints & Seven Angels (14-1-15:4)
    (C$^1$) Seven Bowls (15:1,5-16:21)
  (B$^1$) Seven Angels: whore of Babylon vs. New Jerusalem (17:1-22:5)
(A$^1$) Epilogue (22:6-21)

Source: Nils Wilhelm Lund – 1942

This last but certainly not least astonishing New Testament Nugget of Hebrew Gold is but a forerunner of that which is to come in Section Two of this work. But by now the careful reader should genuinely appreciate what really went into the Holy Bible to help people better learn, understand, and remember the precious lessons contained therein. Indeed, the Bible is a literary and religious miracle proving that Jesus is the Christ, the son of God and that the lessons He taught, most assuredly, give peace and direction in facing life's challenges!

Again, scripture is the word of God as revealed to His Holy Prophets. Scripture is the mind of God, the very will of God and plan of God unto the salvation of man. Scripture is timeless, as relevant in today's world as it was in ancient times.

The chiastic writing technique you have just been introduced to, or been reminded of, was more of an art than a mere style. It is sacred. - Finally, as understood today, this literary fingerprint confirms that the original authors were from the house of Israel and each one an inspired prophet of God.

Chiasmus in the scriptures deepens the meaning of holy writ within the soul of man. Reading and pondering original scripture; the King James Bible, the original Hebrew or Greek translation enlarges the soul, is accurate, refreshing, guiding, calming, and strengthening to those who partake routinely. Amazing that the technique, style, or God given language and beauty of chiasmus, although right under the reader's very eyes for centuries, remained obscure until Nils Lund's landmark treatise published in 1942.

Frankly speaking, if so-called holy writ does not bear the Hebrew fingerprint of chiasmus, well… perhaps it is not true scripture at all, but simply the teachings of men mingled with a smattering of scripture. We may read and study other kinds of books and fine literature, and as uplifting as they can be, they certainly do not compare with God's Holy Word.

Lastly, with a careful investigation of even the best of books we can discover for ourselves little evidence of true chiastic form. It just is not there. First rate Chiasmus, or *Hebrew Gold* is only found in scripture and writings of Hebrew prophets.

# SECTION TWO

# THE HOLY BIBLE IS THE *STICK OF JUDAH*

# NOW WHAT ABOUT THE *STICK OF JOSEPH?*

The word Bible has its roots from Ancient Greek βιβλία (biblía), plural of βιβλίον (biblíon, "book"). It means *many books* therefore the Holy Bible is a collection several books of revealed scripture - much of it written by Hebrew prophets of God and thus containing many passages replete with the ancient Hebrew (Jewish) writing styles – Chiasmus. This is evidence that the Holy Bible is the *Stick of Judah* referred to by the prophet Ezekiel; so, what was Ezekiel referring to when he declared the *Stick of Joseph* in the same breath? And what of the two sticks or scrolls (the *Stick of Judah* and *Stick of Joseph*), being joined together into one at some future day such as these the latter days?

The Church of Jesus Christ of Latter-day Saints teaches that the Book of Mormon is the Stick of Joseph. A bold doctrine and belief that is true...so where is the evidence, where is the proof? And don't the Latter-day Saints also teach and believe that the Book of Mormon was written by prophets of God who lived throughout the ancient Americas and throughout the Western Hemisphere?

But the Eastern and Western hemispheres are vast oceans apart, and in biblical times next to impossible for ships to voyage between the two! Furthermore, many hundreds of years passed before people of the Eastern Hemisphere even knew about the peoples of the Western Hemisphere. There was no commerce between the old world and the new world until 1492.

So, considering the enormous time and distances between the old world and the ancient Americas, the claim that the Book of Mormon is the very *Stick of Joseph* causes serious reflection. For example, how could the original founders and settlers of the ancient Americas be Hebrew? How did they get to the Americas? What evidence did they leave? Didn't the people who originally populated the Americas migrate from Europe and Asia to the Western Hemisphere by crossing the narrow (51 miles) Bering Strait between Russia and Alaska? We know that the ancient Americans are ancestors of the Hispanic peoples of today and most speak one of many Spanish dialects (due to European conquerors who came later), so how could their original language be Hebrew?

Skepticism aside, the Book of Mormon chronicles the departure of a large group of people from the House of Israel who left the land of Jerusalem during the reign of King Zedekiah, then eight years later built a ship, sailed the mighty deep, and landed somewhere in the ancient Americas.

As far-fetched as this sounds modern day archeological diggings, pyramids, and ancient ruins throughout North and South America have proven the above is arguably the gospel truth. That said, here are a few scriptures from within the pages of the Book of Mormon itself:

*1 Nephi 1 verse 2*

> "Yea, I make a record in the language of my father, which consists of the learning of the Jews and the language of the Egyptians."

And...

*2 Nephi 3:4*

> "For behold, thou art the fruit of my loins; and I am a descendant of Joseph who was carried captive into Egypt. And great were the covenants of the Lord which he made unto Joseph."

Also...

*2 Nephi 33:8*

> "I have charity for the Jew - I say Jew, because I mean them from whence I came."

And...

*2 Nephi 28: 2*

> "And the things which shall be written out of the book shall be of great worth unto the children of men, and especially unto our seed which is a remnant of the house of Israel."

Because of the Book of Mormon and other weighty reasons, Latter-day Saints believe that the people of the ancient Americas did in fact have their beginnings in the Middle Eastern Fertile Crescent and evidence that they migrated from Jerusalem during the time of King Nebuchadnezzar (about 591 B.C.) and landed in the Americas is abundant. Indeed, Hebrew, and reformed Egyptian literary patterns in the Book of Mormon and again the ancient ruins found throughout the Americas are proof positive. Guided by the hand of God, a prophet named Lehi was warned that because of wickedness Jerusalem was to be destroyed and the Jews scattered throughout the entire world. Thousands would be imprisoned, and scores of others murdered. But by the grace of God the prophet Lehi and the people we are now discussing, escaped into the wilderness surrounding Jerusalem. This family was ultimately joined by yet another large Jewish family. Through the Lord's guidance and mercy during an eight-year period of time made their way to the ocean shores where they built a ship and sailed the mighty deep eventually arriving in the Americas.

Not wanting these early refugees to forget the language and teachings of their fathers, the Lord commanded them to bring the five Books of Moses, (records of the Jews engraved upon thin plates of brass), and also a record of the genealogy of Lehi's family, along on the ship. This information plus the story of their harrowing voyage is thrilling history and chronicled within the pages of the book of 1 Nephi in the Book of Mormon. Their records and subsequent history in the Americas give a second powerful witness, (the Holy Bible being the first), that Jesus is the Christ the very son of God that by Him, through Him and because of His Atonement we are saved from eternal death.

The Book of Mormon touches the heart and soul of the reader but is it really true? Are the peoples of the Americas really descended from the house of Israel, (Hebrew), and is there evidence within the pages of the Book of Mormon that it is in fact of Egyptian and Hebrew origin? These are deep and thought-provoking questions, the answers to which a person can only discover through reading, study and then from personal prayer.

Regarding the Hebrew writing style of Chiasmus, and researching the fascinating subject cemented my personal belief that Hebrews of ancient times were extremely diligent regarding the education of their offspring. Children of the day were expected to memorize many passages from the Torah, and perhaps learn and use the unique writing technique presented in Section 1 of this book. And so, if it is a fact that the first successful settlers to the Americas were Hebrew, then that unique writing technique and knowledge of the Torah and its teachings (the Laws of Moses) must have crossed the many waters from the old world to the new in 600 B.C. with Lehi, Nephi, and their families.

Thankfully, and fortunately scriptures being as sacred, they were protected, carefully copied, taught, and passed down through the ages thus preserving the Chiastic style of writing and also Hebrew law in the early Americas.

But let me digress just a moment and add that the peoples of the Book of Mormon arrived in the Americas in three separate migrations from the old world to the new. All are chronicled within the pages of the Book of Mormon. The first group, called the Jaredites, came during the time of the Tower of Babel - when God deliberately confounded the common Adamic language of humanity effectively scattering His children all over the face of the earth.

This first group are thought to have arrived in North America somewhere near the Great Lakes region. A floating convoy of eight semi-submersible, tar-pitched barges driven by the wind and waves conveyed them over the ocean. Unfortunately, during the next several hundred years on this continent, wars, and wickedness among them caused this earliest group's almost entire destruction.

The second immigration, the main focus group of the Book of Mormon, are the people of Lehi and his son Nephi who came to the Americas in 591 B.C. Architectural history proves that they were very industrious and became an extremely numerous people. They built a series of complex highways, huge temples, pyramids, and communities populating the Americas from north to south, plus the islands of the pacific.

The third group who came to the ancient Americas were called the people of Mulek, (the only surviving son of King Zedekiah, the last King of Judah) and migrated to the Americas after the Babylonian conquest of Jerusalem. Their history is also contained in the Book of Mormon, and they eventually merged into and became part of the people of Nephi spoken about earlier.

It is unbelievable, but virtually nothing was known about the people of the ancient Americas or their vast civilizations until they were finally discovered by Christopher Columbus in A.D. 1492 – but apparently this was by design. God, in His infinite wisdom and mercy withheld the knowledge of their existence from the peoples of the Old World so that the people of the New would not be exploited by them.

History shows that after Columbus, came Hernando Cortez followed by swarms of Spanish Conquistadors and in very deed the less educated, less advanced people of the Americas were hugely exploited, religiously, economically, and even healthwise. Measles and other communicable diseases were devastating to the formerly isolated peoples. The preceding brief explanation notwithstanding let us continue...

To begin, there are definitely Chiasmus within the pages of the Book of Mormon...scores of them. The Book of Mormon covers over one thousand years of history in the ancient Americas and remarkably as time passed the literary science of Chiastic style remains solidly throughout.

Only in the Book of Ether is the Chiastic technique absent, but when one understands that this unique document – The Book of Ether – began recording history during the time of the Tower of Babel and concluded before anyone with a background in the Hebrew language arrived in the Americas, it makes perfect sense.

One more comment before we continue; Chiasmus' in the Book of Mormon are much clearer than those found in the King James Version of the Holy Bible. This is simply because the Book of Mormon has had a single translation from the original Reformed Egyptian and Hebrew languages into English, whereas there were many translations of the Holy Bible before King James scholars even began the monumental task of bringing the best of these translations together in a single volume of scripture.

There is no criticism here, just fact and thank God for the precious King James Bible because of the attempts made to destroy the work. It is nothing short of a miracle that we have this mighty volume of Holy Scripture to guide us and to testify of the reality of the Lord Jesus Christ.

The following pages contain eight Chiasmus examples copied from the Book of Mormon:

# 1 Nephi 15: 9-11

9. And they said unto me: We have not; for the Lord maketh no such thing known unto us.
10. Behold, I said unto them: How is it that ye do not keep the commandments of the Lord? How is it that ye will perish, because of the hardness of your hearts?
11. Do ye not remember the things which the Lord hath said? – If ye will not harden your hearts, and ask me in faith, believing that ye shall receive, with diligence in keeping my commandments, surely these things shall be made known unto you.

**A** And they said unto me: We have not; for the Lord maketh no such thing known unto us.

    **B** Behold, I said unto them: How is it that ye do not keep the commandments of the Lord?

        **C** How is it that ye will perish,

            **D** because of the hardness of your hearts?

            **D¹** . . . If ye will not harden your hearts,

        **C¹** and ask me in faith, believing that ye shall receive,

    **B¹** with diligence in keeping my commandments,

**A¹** surely these things shall be made known unto you.

The above scripture diagrammed reveals a perfectly balanced Chiastic structure, a completed thought pattern, and powerfully intensified meaning within. Indeed the very reason for the science or call it the art of Chiasmus.

 **2 Nephi 29:13**

13. And it shall come to pass that the Jews shall have the words of the Nephites, and the Nephites shall have the words of the Jews; and the Nephites and the Jews shall have the words of the lost tribes of Israel; and the lost tribes of Israel shall have the words of the Nephites and Jews.

## 2 Nephi 29:13 (diagrammed)

**A** The Jews

   **B** shall have the words

      **C** of the Nephites,

      **C¹** and the Nephites

   **B¹** shall have the words

**A¹** of the Jews.


**A** And the Nephites and the Jews

   **B** shall have the words

      **C** of the lost tribes of Israel;

      **C¹** and the lost tribes of Israel

   **B¹** shall have the words

**A¹** of the Nephites and the Jews.

Again, the preceding scriptural diagrams reveal perfect Chiastic structure common in the writings of Hebrew trained prophets of God. Yet they were revealed and recorded oceans away from Jerusalem and the old world, they were recorded in the Americas, the new world.

# King Benjamin

Before his famous address in the Book of Mosiah, could it have been possible that this humble king had his Hebrew-trained scribes write and produce copies of it for his people?

It is not only possible but highly likely because even though this great King spoke from a tower to hundreds of his people camped below on the gentle inclines of a huge valley, the year was 124 B.C. and the world had to wait thousands of years before the invention of public address systems.

Most certainly King Benjamin's famous address was written out before he delivered it because throughout his discourse when parts of it are diagrammed some of the most perfect Chiasmus appear.

On the next page are copies of two pages from the Book of Mormon. On the left is a copy from the original 1830 edition, while the page on the right is a copy from the 2018 or current edition. Both pages highlight <u>Mosiah Chapter 3 verses 18 and 19</u> two of my favorite scriptures.

For clarity and comparison, I have copied the highlighted scripture in both the 1830 edition and in the modern edition. Magnify the pages* (they are clear on Power Point) and see if you can pick up a Chiastic pattern as you read either or both. Again, be reminded that the Book of Mormon was first published in 1830 and that Chiasmus were not recognized or recorded until Bible scholar Nils W. Lund discovered them and published his book 'Chiasmus in the New Testament' in the year of our Lord 1942, one hundred and twelve years after the first printing of the Book of Mormon.

The modern edition of the Book of Mormon is edited into paragraphs with added references below. Note that there are no changes in wording between the old and the new editions.

# BOOK OF MORMON:

# 1830 Edition vs Current Edition

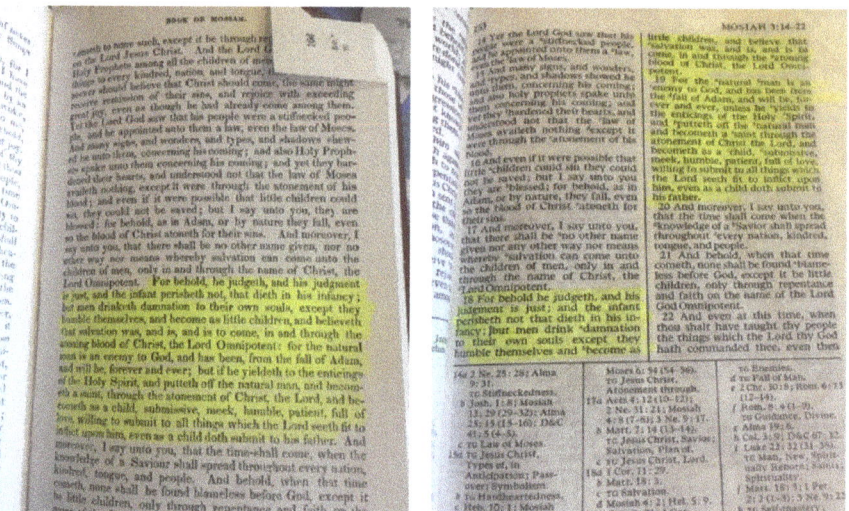

Oddly enough, scholars from the Church of Jesus Christ of Latter-day Saints had not made any reference to Chiasmus in the Book of Mormon until the early 1960's, overlooking the science almost entirely, and it is obvious that Joseph Smith and Oliver Cowdery his scribe, much less anyone else in 1830 knew anything about Chiasmus.

*Hebrew Gold* was originally presented on a Power Point presentation, therefore please accept the author's apology, that magnification is needed here. The pages are available in a copy of the original 1830 Book of Mormon as well as the modern day's sectioned and referenced copy.

## Mosiah Chapter 3 verses 18 and 19

18. But men drink damnation to their own souls except they humble themselves and become as little children, and believe that salvation was, and is, and is to come in and through the atoning blood of Christ, the Lord Omnipotent.

19. For the natural man is an enemy to God, and has been from the fall of Adam, and will be forever and ever, unless he yields to the enticings of the holy spirit and putteth off the natural man and becometh a saint through the atonement of Christ the Lord, and becometh as a child, submissive, meek, humble, patient, full of love, willing to submit to all things which the Lord seeth fit to inflict upon him, even as a child doth submit to his father.

...but men drink damnation to their own souls except

**A**   they humble themselves

    **B**   and become as little children,

       **C**   and believe that salvation . . . is. . . in and through the atoning blood of Christ, the Lord Omnipotent.

         **D**   For the natural man

           **E**   is an enemy to God,

             **F**   and has been from the fall of Adam,

             **F¹**   and will be forever and ever,

           **E¹**   unless he yields to the enticings of the holy spirit,

         **D¹**   and putteth off the natural man

       **C¹**   and becometh a saint through the atonement of Christ the Lord,

    **B¹**   and becometh as a child,

**A¹**   submissive, meek, humble . . . full of love . . . .

To see and feel the strength and beauty of a diagrammed Chiasmus more poignantly read A then A' then B then B' then C and C' etc. all the way to the central message.

The foregoing diagrammed Chiasmus contains a perfect pattern of speech, precise in meaning, complete in thought, and presents a powerful scriptural message from a prophet of God who lived in the ancient Americas 124 years before the time of Christ. Here is another:

# Mosiah 5:10-12

10. And now it shall come to pass, that whosoever shall not take upon him the name of Christ must be called by some other name; therefore, he findeth himself on the left hand of God.

11. And I would that ye should remember also, that this is the name that never should be blotted out, except it be through transgression; therefore, take heed that ye do not transgress, that the name be not blotted out of your hearts.

> **A**   And now . . . whosoever shall not take upon him the name of Christ
>> **B**   must be called by some other name;
>>> **C**   therefore he findeth himself on the left hand of God.
>>>> **D**   I would that ye should remember also, that this is the name . . .
>>>>> **E**   that never should be blotted out,
>>>>>> **F**   except it be through transgression;
>>>>>> **F¹**   therefore, take heed that ye do not transgress,
>>>>> **E¹**   that the name be not blotted out of your hearts.
>>>> **D¹**   I would that ye should remember to retain the name.
>>> **C¹**   that ye are not found on the left hand of God,
>> **B¹**   but that ye hear and know the voice by which ye shall be called,
> **A¹**   and also, the name by which He shall call you.

12. I would that ye should remember to retain the name that ye are not found on the left hand of God, but that ye hear and

know the voice by which ye shall be called, and also, the name by which He shall call you.

## The entire Book of Mosiah is a Chiasmus!

(A) King Benjamin exhorts his sons (1:1-8)
 (B) Mosiah chosen king to succeed his father (1:10)
  (C) Mosiah receives the records (1:16)
   (D) Benjamin's speech and the words of an angel of the Lord (2:9 – 5:15)
    (E) People enter into a covenant (6:1)
     (F) Priests consecrated (6:3)
      (G) Ammon leaves Zarahemla for the land of Lehi-Nephi (7:1-6)
       (H) People of Limhi in bondage; Ammon put in prison (7:15)
        (I) The 24 gold plates (8:9)
         (J) The record of Zeniff begins as he leaves Zarahemla (9:1)
          (K) Zeniff prevails against the Lamanites (9:14 – 10:20)
           (L) Noah and his priests (11:1-15)
            (M) Abinadi persecuted and thrown in prison (11-12)
             (N) Abinadi reads Isaiah's prophecies of Christ (13-14)
             (N¹) Abinadi makes his own prophecies of Christ (15-16)
            (M¹) Abinadi persecuted and killed (17:5-20)
           (L¹) Noah and his priests (18:32 – 20:5)
          (K¹) Lamanites threaten the people of Limhi (20:6-26)
         (J¹) Record of Zeniff ends as Limhi's people leave the land of Lehi-Nephi
        (I¹) The 24 gold plates (21:27, 22:14)
       (H¹) People of Alma in bondage (23)
      (G¹) Alma leaves the land of Lehi-Nephi for Zarahemla (24)
     (F¹) The Church organized by Alma (25:14-24)
    (E¹) Unbelievers refuse to enter covenant (26:1-4)
   (D¹) The words of Alma and the words of an angel of the Lord (26-27)
  (C¹) Alma the Younger receives the records (28:20)
 (B¹) Judges chosen instead of a king (29:5-32)
(A¹) Mosiah exhorts his people (29:5-32).

Source: John W. Welch, "Chiasmus in the Book of Mormon" BYU Studies Autumn 1969

Time to pause and reflect; in 1830, when The Book of Mormon was first published, virtually nothing was known about the Chiastic literary style. Dr. Nils Wilhelm Lund's discovery of the science, or art if you will, did not happen until 1938 and again it wasn't until 1942 did his published work appear. I have said it before but again, that was 112 years after the first printing of the Book of Mormon.

To continue, the next scripture from the book of Alma becomes a compound Chiasmus when diagrammed:

# Alma 41:13-14

13.  O, my son, this is not the case; but the meaning of the word restoration is to bring back again evil for evil, or carnal for carnal, or devilish for devilish– good for that which is good; righteous for that which is righteous; just for that which is just; merciful for that which is merciful.

14.  Therefore, my son, see that you are merciful unto your brethren; deal justly, judge righteously, and do good continually; and if ye do all these things then shall ye receive your reward; yea, ye shall have mercy restored unto you again; ye shall have a righteous judgment restored unto you again; and ye shall have good rewarded unto you again.

(diagrammed)

**A**   GOOD for that which is GOOD;

   **B**   RIGHTEOUS for that which is RIGHTEOUS;

      **C**   JUST for that which is JUST;

         **D**   MERCIFUL for that which is MERCIFUL.

         **D¹**   Therefore, my son, see that you are MERCIFUL unto your brethren;

      **C¹**   deal JUSTLY,

   **B¹**   judge RIGHTEOUSLY,

**A¹**   and do GOOD continually; and if ye do all these things then shall ye receive your reward;

         **D²**   yea, ye shall have MERCY restored unto you again,

      **C²**   ye shall have JUSTICE restored unto you again;

   **B²**   ye shall have a RIGHTEOUS judgment restored unto you again;

**A²**   and ye shall have GOOD rewarded unto you again.

And …

# Alma 41:13-14 (expanded - simplified)

**A** And now behold, is the meaning of the word restoration to take a thing of a natural state and place it in an unnatural state, or to place it in a state opposite to its nature? O, my son, this is not the case; but the meaning of the word restoration is to bring back again evil for evil, canal for carnal, or devilish for devilish -

**B** GOOD for that which is GOOD;

**C** RIGHTEOUS for that which is RIGHTEOUS;

**D** JUST for that which is JUST;

**E** MERCIFUL for that which is MERCIFUL.

**E¹** Therefore, my son, see that you are MERCIFUL unto your brethren;

**D¹** deal JUSTLY,

**C¹** judge RIGHTEOUSLY,

**B¹** and do GOOD continually;

**A¹** and if ye do all these things then shall ye receive your reward; yea, ye shall have mercy restored unto you again; ye shall have justice restored unto you again; ye shall have a righteous judgment restored unto you again; and ye shall have good rewarded unto you again. For that which ye do send out shall return unto you again, and be restored; therefore, the word restoration more fully condemneth the sinner, and justifieth him not at all.

Source: Steven D. Nielsen - 2017

# Alma Chapter 36:

# A Masterpiece of Hebrew Writing Style

(A) My son, give ear to my **WORDS** (1)
  (B) **KEEP THE COMMANDMENTS** of God and ye shall **PROSPER IN THE LAND** (2)
    (C) **DO AS I HAVE DONE** (2)
      (D) in **REMEMBERING THE CAPTIVITY** of our fathers (2);
        (E) for they were in **BONDAGE** (2)
          (F) he surely did **DELIVER** them (2)
            (G) **TRUST** in God (3)
              (H) supported in their **TRIALS, and TROUBLES, and AFFLICTIONS** (3)
                (I) shall be lifted up at the **LAST DAY** (3)
                  (J) I **KNOW** this not of myself but of **GOD** (4)
                    (K) **BORN OF GOD** (5)
                      (L) I sought to destroy the church of God (6-9)
                        (M) **MY LIMBS** were paralyzed (10)
                          (N) Fear of being in the **PRESENCE OF GOD** (14-15)
                            (O) **PAINS** of a damned soul (16)
                              (P) **HARROWED UP BY THE MEMORY OF SINS** (17)
                                (Q) I remembered **JESUS CHRIST, SON OF GOD** (17)
                                (Q') I cried, **JESUS, SON OF GOD** (18)
                              (P') **HARROWED UP BY THE MEMORY OF SINS** no more
                            (O') Joy as exceeding as was the **PAIN** (20)
                        (N') Long to be in the **PRESENCE OF GOD** (22)
                        (M') My **LIMBS** received their strength again (23)
                    (L') I labored to bring souls to repentance (24)
                (K') **BORN OF GOD** (26)
                (J') Therefore **MY KNOWLEDGE IS OF GOD** (26)
              (I') and **RAISE ME UP AT THE LAST DAY** (28)
            (H') supported under **TRIALS, TROUBLES, and AFFLICTIONS** (27)
          (G') **TRUST** in him (27 )
        (F') He will deliver me (27)
      (E') As God brought our fathers out of **BONDAGE** and captivity (28-29)
    (D') Retain in **REMEMBRANCE THEIR CAPTIVITY** (28-29)
  (C') **KNOW AS I DO KNOW** (30)
 (B') **KEEP THE COMMANDMENTS** and ye shall **PROSPER IN THE LAND** (30)
(A') This is according to his **WORD** (30).

Source: John W. Welch, "What Does Chiasmus in the Book of Mormon Prove?" F.A.R.M.S., pp. 200-224

# CONCLUSION –

 **Scriptures are Revelations from God our Heavenly Father to His prophets**

The top two pictures depict Old and New Testament prophets of the Holy Bible, Moses, Aaron, and Isaiah… and the bottom two pictures are of the golden plates (containing the entire Book of Mormon) and of the ancient American prophet Moroni. The bottom right-hand picture is of the latter-day prophet Joseph Smith Jr. who translated the Book of Mormon from Reformed Egyptian /Hebrew into English.

Joseph Smith's life was truly remarkable but also short-lived wherein and through powers from on high the true Church of Jesus Christ was once again established upon the earth. Remarkably, the fledgling church grew from just six initial members in 1830 to somewhere north of 100,000 souls in 1844 when Smith was martyred. An utterly astounding feat considering the fact that the telegraph was in  its infancy, there were no telephones much less any form of mass communication media other than newspapers and the horse and buggy or simply walking provided people of the day the transportation needed to get around. Indeed, information of any kind spread painfully slowly.

## Joseph Smith – What are the facts?

- Born December 23rd, 1805 Died June 27th, 1844
- Translated The Book of Mormon from Hebrew and Reformed Egyptian during a period of 90 days give or take.
- Published the Book of Mormon during the year 1830 when he was just 24 years old.

Joseph Smith was hated and persecuted by men of the cloth, certain politicians, and many others under their persuasions and influence. He was mobbed, beaten, tarred & feathered, spit upon, arrested, jailed, and often dragged into court on false pretenses from the time he first received the gold plates, (in 1827), upon which the Book of Mormon was recorded, until the day of his murder on June 27, 1844 – during his 38th year of life.

Was he a true prophet of God? I testify that he was. I testify that through him God and His son Jesus The Christ performed a mighty work and a wonder, the restoration of Christ's true church upon the earth.

A humble farm boy, typical of the time with limited education and opportunity, the translation of the Book of Mormon and the resulting spread of the Gospel of Jesus Christ is a miracle! And a careful study of the Book of Mormon and the Holy Bible prove that true prophets of God recorded both. Men called before the foundation of the world was even laid; Moses, Isaiah, Jeremiah, Ezekiel, Paul, Nephi, Mosiah, Alma, etc. and yes, even Joseph Smith, mortal men called and set apart by God as His true prophets.

## Joseph Smith – in Emma's words

Emma Smith, the wife of Joseph's youth, and the woman who knew him best, recorded the following in a letter in1847:

> *"My husband could neither write nor dictate a coherent and well-worded letter, let alone write a book like the Book of Mormon.*

> *He was 23 years old and when acting as his scribe, Joseph would dictate to me hour after hour; and when returning after meals, or after interruptions, he would at once begin where he had left off, without either seeing the manuscript or having any portion of it read back to him. This was the usual thing for him to do. It would have been improbable that a learned man could do this; and, for one so ignorant and unlearned as he was, it was simply impossible."*

For a brief time, Emma acted as Joseph's first scribe but their children, her household and garden - in those days critical for family survival - proved daunting indeed and Emma gladly relinquished her duties as a scribe turning the job over to a schoolteacher named Oliver Cowdery from Vermont who had recently arrived in Manchester, from upstate New York. Cowdery age 24, became a lodger with various families in the area, including that of Joseph Smith's father and mother.

From then on, the translation of the 588 pages that comprise the Book of Mormon, happened rapidly, taking approximately 90 days to complete. When published by the E.B. Grandin & Company of Palmyra New York in 1830, it provided the foundation for the greatest force for good on the face of the earth today, the Church of Jesus Christ of Latter-day Saints.

Called the most perfect book on the earth, the Book of Mormon has changed the lives of millions for the better. Those who have read and continue to read and study, proclaim it to be a book of pure truth and direction, indeed a "Marvelous Work and a Wonder."

The translation and publication of the Book of Mormon occurred when Joseph Smith was in his early twenties. He had had but a few years of formal schooling and was barely able to spell much less write lengthy communications; but let it not be said that Joseph Smith remained uneducated and unlearned. From 1830, just twenty-five years old when the Church of Jesus Christ of Latter-day Saints was first organized and throughout his short life the young prophet was tutored by the likes of Peter, James, and John and several other prophets of the Holy Scriptures. Lastly, the Lord Jesus Christ also thoroughly schooled him.

Naturally skeptics bristle and chide at this candid, complimentary portrayal, but the facts remain that before his murder by a mob at a jail in Carthage, Illinois, (at the age of 38), Joseph Smith had become a very proficient writer, community organizer, councilor, and leader of men. Yet he remained a humble, teachable, and loving person; a kind and generous individual who led the fledgling church by revelation directly from God, and His Son Jesus Christ.

And Jesus Christ is the very head and chief cornerstone of the Church of Jesus Christ of Latter-day Saints under whose guidance and direction through modern-day prophets has flourished and is flourishing. Members today are found throughout the world and number nearly seventeen million!

But back to the subject of this treatise. There are many articles,  essays and political speeches written and presented today whose authors use techniques vaguely similar to Chiastic form. Seasoned speech writers and orators understand the power of repetition of ideas and key points to strengthen and put across their messages. *But pure Hebrew Chiastic form is definitely absent.* Modern text bears little or no similarity to finely structured Hebrew writ found in ancient scripture as recorded by Hebrew Prophets; such Chiasmus as found in the Holy Bible and in the Book of Mormon. Regardless, blessed are they who immerse themselves within the pages of Holy Scripture both modern day and ancient.

Diligent scripture study gives a sure mental foundation and peace of mind. Many students of holy writ give sincere thanks in  prayer for the prophets who sacrificed so much (even their very lives), to bring the Holy Bible and the Book of Mormon into our hands. Both canons of scripture complement one another perfectly. Both are of Hebrew origin, and both are sacred. Passed down to us, the Holy Bible and the Book of Mormon enrich our lives and bring us joy and direction. The prophesy found in Ezekiel 37 has been fulfilled; The Stick of Judah and The Stick of Joseph have literally become one and are available to *all of God's children...* available to you!

# EPILOGUE

Did Moses, a Hebrew prophet really part the Red Sea in the old world? Were his writings Chiastic in structure? Was he led by God through revelation? Did his teachings influence the likes of Abraham, Isaac, Jacob and eventually all the 12 Tribes of Israel?

And as Moses prophesied, did Jesus Christ, the only begotten Son of God really walk among the progeny of the House of Israel? Does the Holy Bible itself contain true human history? Or are the stories within its page's mere fables?

Did Christ really heal the sick, raise the dead, give sight to the blind and were His teachings given to the entire world – the peoples of both the Eastern and the Western Hemispheres? Were His words those of God our Heavenly Father? Did Christ really agonize and bleed at every pore in the Garden of Gethsemane on our behalf? Was He then crucified upon the cruel slopes of Golgotha for the express purpose of atoning for the sins of all mankind?

Was Jesus Christ then the first fruits of the Resurrection? And did He appear to the people of both the Eastern and the Western Hemispheres? Will we ourselves be resurrected?

Significant questions. Are the Holy Bible *and* the Book of Mormon true scripture written by true prophets of God? Will reading and studying these documents of scripture help bring us closer to our Heavenly Father and His Son the Lord Jesus Christ? Will scripture study improve your life? Give you better direction and more peace of mind? In a word, absolutely.

But concerning the very root of the Chiasmus structure found within holy scripture, and how it got there – was it careful planning, deep consideration, prophet forethought or simply a skill taught in Hebrew schools and homes? My personal belief is none of the above. All things considered; the very length of some Chiasmus,' including entire chapters and books, plus the sheer number of them in the scriptures compel me to believe that the true source of the *Chiastic structure*, plus the poetic beauty and sweetness found within the holy scriptures, originally tumbled down from the very lips of almighty God.

The physical evidence, either linguistic evidence such as the ancient Hebrew writing styles you have just studied, or the archeological ruins found throughout the holy land and in the Americas is helpful in believing. But these evidences will not always give a *spiritual witness* as will actually *reading* the truths presented within Holy Scripture and then praying about them.

As stated earlier, there are people even believe that the Bible consists of fables, made up stories written by old men calling themselves prophets. Worse has been said concerning the Book of Mormon. Nevertheless, and specifically concerning scripture, the fact is that God has given us the very power to dispel all doubt and know if it is true. That power is the power of prayer. It is that simple. We can pray and receive answers to the afore stated questions, and any to other questions we may have throughout our lives. Answers directly from God. For instance, consider the book of James, Chapter 1: verses 5 and 6:

*"If any of you lack wisdom, let him ask of God, that giveth to all men liberally, and upbraideth not; and it shall be given him. But let him ask in faith, nothing wavering…"*

To find out if the Book of Mormon, and for that matter the Holy Bible, contain the true word of God, a person must first read them. Read a few pages, read a few chapters… and then pray to God our Heavenly Father. Ask Him and He will answer.

*"And when ye shall receive these things, I would exhort you that ye would <u>ask God</u>, the Eternal Father, in the name of Christ, if these things are not true; and if ye shall ask with a sincere heart, with real intent, having faith in Christ, he will manifest the truth of it unto you, by the power of the Holy Ghost. And by the power of the Holy Ghost ye may know the truth of all things."* Book of Mormon, Moroni Chapter 10: verses 4 and 5.

That is quite a promise, but you have everything to gain and nothing to lose by putting it to the test. Read the Book of Mormon, (also read the Holy Bible if you have not already done so) and then find a quiet place where you can be alone for a while and take the challenge. Kneel and ask God in the name of Christ, if what you have read is true, but ask in faith, nothing wavering… And you will know the truth for yourself, *count on it.*

It is my testimony that the Book of Mormon is true. Like the Holy Bible it is the word of God. I know it and have this testimony confirmed to me each time I read and ponder the teachings contained therein. I am enriched, given strength and direction, and most importantly, given to know that Jesus is the Christ, the very Son of God the Savior and Redeemer of all humanity.

It is my further testimony that the Book of Mormon and the Holy Bible go hand in hand in perfect harmony and because of the teachings within them I am a blessed individual, supremely grateful for life and whatever brings to me.

In the Holy name of our Savior, Jesus Christ, Amen.

# ADDITIONAL INFORMATION

As a sidenote, experts in the field of Mesoamerican languages and texts have also discovered Chiasmus within the pages of certain ancient Mayan writings. This fact pleased me but did not really surprise me, because the Mayans were also ancestors of the original Hebrew settlers to the Americas - but now we are getting off point.

Suffice it to say an excellent article titled "Chiasmus in Mayan Texts" written by a translator of ancient Indian languages of Guatemala, one Allen J. Christianson is readily available on the internet, as are every resource material supporting this work. There is a great deal of information on Chiasmus on the internet, mountains of it.

While it goes without saying that the people chronicled within the pages of the Holy Bible populated parts of the <u>Eastern Hemisphere</u>; fought wars there, built buildings there, lived and died there… so also there is ample archeological and written evidence proving beyond a shadow of doubt of the existence of an ancient, highly intelligent population that inhabited the <u>Western Hemisphere</u>.

New discoveries on both hemispheres of our beautiful Earth present further *archeological* evidence of these truths. That said, the book you hold in your hands gives *linguistic* evidence that people on the Eastern Hemisphere and those on the Western Hemisphere sprang from a common heredity.

# REFERENCES

Dr. Nils Wilhelm Lund - Chiasmus in the New Testament – Published 1942.

Dr. James Boyer - Greek Exegetical Methods -1973-1974.

John W. Welch, PhD."Chiasmus in the Book of Mormon" BYU Studies Autumn 1969.

John W. Welch, "What Does Chiasmus in the Book of Mormon Prove?" F.A.R.M.S., pp. 200-224.

Emma Smith - Last Testimony of Emma Smith 1879 Q&A between Emma and Joseph Smith III, The Saints' Herald 26 (Oct 1879).

Letter of Lewis C. Bidamon to Emma Smith dated 11 January 1847, (Department of History, Community of Christ, Independence, Missouri.).

Thomas B. Clarke - Two Examples That Help Explain Chiastic Structures.

Orchard Keeper - article by John Baumgardner.

Menorah Format – James N. Hall 2011.

# INFORMATION OF INTEREST

Menorah: A pattern of thought written out that tends to repeat certain ideas in an effort to strengthen or clarify meaning.

Menorahs are common throughout recorded literature and not found exclusively in any one type of author, or people or specific religion.

A Menorah is not a Chiasmus of words or phrases or grammatical fragments. A Menorah is an inverted parallelism of thought of concepts. A seven holder Hebrew candelabra as shown below, is also called a Menorah.

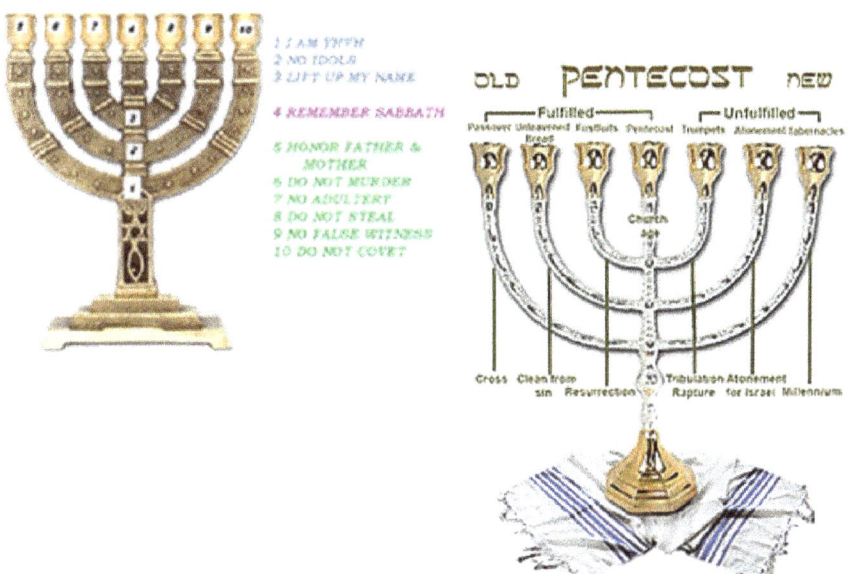

www.ingramcontent.com/pod-product-compliance
Lightning Source LLC
Chambersburg PA
CBHW051237120626
46547CB00013B/1691